May 2003

For Dave,

I wish ████████ ...e
best, and know you'll
do great things !!
With Love, ☺
Kirsten

What Learning Leaves

What Learning Leaves

Taylor Mali

4.15.03

Hanover Press, Ltd.
Newtown, CT

WHAT LEARNING LEAVES

Book Design and Production: David Martin

Published in the United States by

Hanover Press, Ltd.
P.O. Box 596
Newtown, CT 06470-0596

Manufactured in the United States of America.

ISBN   1-887012-17-6

for Rebecca

Contents

The body craves

Going on from there

Next stop

That's me at the front of the subway train
with my face pressed up against the glass
watching as every oncoming red light
goes green then slides on past.

My hands are cupped round my eyes,
and my back is to the rest of the car.
If I block out the light from where I am
standing, I can see just as far

as the bends in tracks will allow me.
Silent whistle or unlit beacon:
here I am at the front of the train
staring forward as if I were seeking

for the color and texture of darkness,
or how a broken heart becomes whole,
the here and now of the future,
the exact size and shape of the soul.

There are others who do as I do:
who stand here and strain to see.
Granted they're usually 10 years old
but that doesn't bother me

because I have my back to the subway car
and my face pressed up to the glass,
and every red light will eventually change
to green, then slide on past.

Three-hole punches

First day of school

This is it, the most important moment,
the original transgression.
If this were writing, this would be the opening line
(except you'd be able to go back
and change it if you didn't get it right).
If this were love at first sight,
this would be the moment you bumped into each other,
the night you began your mutual confessions.

It's time to recalibrate and revise
the rambling digression of summer eyes
and focus on a more decorous expression —
say, the red and yellow leaves of trees
that have scattered themselves all over the lawn
with abandon and indiscretion.

With abandon and indiscretion
be like early autumn air and freshen.
Because school is now in session
and you know the old expression,
you never get a second chance to make a first impression.

What learning leaves

My children have all gone home
leaving me with nothing to do
but grade, plan, record, worry,
and call their parents.

Jenny' s mother ends the conversation by telling me
that I seem like the only teacher who understands
that learning is fun,
that it should leave you feeling refreshed.

I look around my room and think,
in the parlance of the sixth grade, *no way*!
Learning is tiring, frustrating, often boring,
and as for feeling refreshed, their blood sugar levels
are so low by three o'clock that the only thing
my students have the energy to do
is beat each other up and scream.

Refreshed is not on the list of what learning leaves.
What is you ask?

Overturned desks and tipped over chairs
as if learning does damage before finally coming to rest.
Staples and mangled paper clips, no longer able
to hold anything together.
Pencils dulled by sleep or splintered by imagination,
some too short to sharpen, but still too long to throw away.

Pens! Hundreds of pens.
Most of them almost empty, chewed at the ends,
barely capable of writing.

Used Kleenex. Learning leaves wads of it
all around my classroom. Because learning produces snot.
It's what lubricates the educated mind.
Learning is messy and disgusting.

And let's not forget the paper.
Handouts and class notes from mine and other classes.
Unused sheets of lined paper,
gum wrappers and Pokemon cards,
hundreds of little three-hole punches,
the disgruntled homework in the trash can,
always the bad grades, the crumpled quiz that
failed by please, please, please . . .
just five, four, three . . . two points.
Learning grows as a tree, from a rustling pile of loose leaves.

This is the wake of my teaching;
this mess tells me I'm doing something right.
I can't get to sleep on Sunday night.
I'm wasted like the unused piece of paper in the trash can,
like the pen with chewed ends, almost incapable of writing.
And inside my mind there are overturned desks
and partly erased blackboards.

Poet teaching math and history

I'm the one they come to when they need to know
if history is positive or negative,
if math rhymes,
if poetry is odd or if it's just poets who are.
Because those who do not know poetry
will be doomed to repeat it.

Pop Quiz:
Who won the Battle of the Imagination?
What makes people think π is easy?
True or False: Power corrupts and metaphoric
power corrupts metaphorically.
How many poems were martyred in the Coliseum,
fed to ferocious perpendicular lions?
Do equilateral triangles ever fall in love with squares?
Take all the problems in the world.
Solve.
Be sure to calculate your answer in number sentences.

Word Problem:
If an elephant begins crossing the Alps going south
while at the exact same time the number five begins
writing a metaphor in the opposite direction,
how long will it take for the word love
to round itself off to the nearest poem?

Extra Credit Question:
What's b plus b? (2b)
That's not the question. What's 2b times 2? (4b)
What's 4b x 11c? (44bc)
Friends, Romans, Countrymen;
Show none of your work all of the time
because all of life's a make-up test,
and all roads lead to rhyme.

The wisest woman in the eighth grade

I tell Diana I am teaching at an all boy's school
and she tells me she thought I knew better.

You of all people, Mr. Mali.
I would have thought you had learned by now
that Girls Rule.

I want to say, "What makes you think I haven't?"
Or perhaps, "What makes you think you didn't
teach me that lesson yourself?" Or perhaps . . .

No. I have to remember that this is the girl
who held my hand on the camping trip
to keep her balance when she sneezed
and said, *If it's true what they say —*
that sex is better than this —
then I can hardly wait.

Perhaps it was then I understood
how close we live to serious disciplinary action.
How rarely are we more than a sentence away
from chaos, tears, emotional wrecks and wrecked careers.
We haul the barges of our own destruction
behind us with lines we never throw out.

Words have power. Not like engines, like atoms.
You can split your whole life apart
if you gather all the wrong words together in the right place.
Even a single letter can work wonders
if you write it well and mean it.

So even though I teach
at an all boys school now,
God bless you, Diana.
God bless you.

Please see me

If all the year were playing holidays,
To sport would be as tedious as to work;
But when they seldom come, they wish'd for come,
And nothing pleaseth but rare accidents.
— Henry IV, Part 1

And speaking of rare accidents, come in,
shuck off your book bag, please, pull up a chair.
Let me tell you why I didn't grade your paper.
See, you're either average or lazy,
and you better know which one you are
because I'm sick of hearing, "I didn't understand!
I don't know why," when the truth is, "I don't care,
and I didn't even try."

I know you all.

You'd rather be suspected of being stupid,
because you know you're not,
than be accused of being lazy, because you know you are.
I don't think you're stupid,
but if you expected me to fall for that,
then maybe I am wrong.

Which is to say, this is not your best work.
I'm not asking you to write the paper over again
unless you deleted the file after printing it, in which case,
I'm asking you to write the paper over again.

Look at the next lines:
When this loose behavior I throw off
And pay the debt I never promised,
By how much better than my word I am,
By so much shall I falsify men's hopes.

That's what you're doing, isn't it?
You're getting by at four so that when you turn up the volume
you can go all the way to eight and I'll be impressed.

10

But life goes to eleven, baby.
And then it keeps on going.
So tell me I ain't seen nothing yet.
Tell me you can do much better than this.
Falsify my hopes and shine.
Otherwise you'll always be what you are now:
dismissed.

Gene pool

for Lawrence Brown

One question for the clucking parents
of the genius in my class:

How could such an eagle of a child
have such chickens for parents?

Playing Scrabble with Eddie

Despite his dyslexia or perhaps because of it,
Eddie can beat every other eighth grader in Scrabble.
Kick their asses in fact, and he knows it,
though he can't say it, at least not in those words,
because if he said "ass" in my eighth grade
I'd give him a detention on the spot.

Scrabble was made for his mind.
Show him a rack of seven letters,
he'll tell you in an instant 10 different words
that use some combination of those letters,
his mind hard-wired for confusion,
for discombobulating vowels
and the jangling clangor of consonants.
But ask him to spell those 10 words,
and he may DARE to READ DEAR
when the word READS DREAD.

Combine dyslexia with hyperactivity,
which now we call A.D.D.,
Attention Deficit Disorder,—
though Eddie says impishly, D.D.A.!—
fifteen milligrams of Ritalin taken twice a day,
dispensed by the nurse, an IQ of 165
and all the hormones of a 13-year-old boy
just dying for an education, and you have yourself
one horny, whacked-out, eighth-grade genius
staring at the seven tiles on his rack
as if getting the letters in the right order
would unlock all the secrets of the language.

Eddie stares at my face, at the board, at his rack,
at his rack, at the board, at my face.
And I wonder what his dyslexic, rearranging mind
is doing with my eyes & my ears & my nose.

How many one-eyed, Picasso-faced English teachers
are staring back at him from the educated
audience of his adolescence?
How many monsters can he spell with my face?
But here comes the word:

    K-C-U-F.

Kcuf? Eddie, I think I'm going to have to
challenge you on this word.

And Eddie reddens. Eddie reddens
like he finally got the punch line to a dirty Joke,
which in a way he has. Eddie reddens
like I've finally caught him swearing,
which in a way I haven't. Yet.

And the letters pivot around the K.

    C-U-F.

Oh. Well, that's different.

    "Is that okay, Mr. Mali?"

Is that okay!? Is that okay, Eddie!?
You landed the F on a Double Letter square
and the K on a Double Word—
That's 34 points, young man!

    "Hot shit!" says Eddie.

And I give him a detention on the spot.

As far as words go, or,
How to revise your paper

First of all, find a better title.
And make it more like yourself,
inventive, a bit punchy,
but good at heart.

The real problem is
you're not telling me enough
about far too much.

So reach for the pen,
the one with ink as red as your blood
is blue,
and tell me much more,
but about much less.

Sharpen your mind as if it were a pencil;
whet and hone it to its finest point.
Then as you write press harder,
write deeper.

Leave the imprint of your words
so that they can still be read on the
under pages of a loose leaf pad.

If some of your sentences are long, amusing puzzles
with a syntactic complexity that rivals the brain,
make others short.

If your paper were to catch fire,
make your introduction the paragraph
you would rush to save first.

And as far as words go,
mix the luscious Latinate ones
with spicy bits and gritty chunks
of good Germanic stuff.
Luxuriate in the romance of all languages;
make them all your own tongue.

Revise and rewrite, and switch around and scratch things out
(using carets, arrows, and asterisks)
until you stumble at last on the eloquent.

Paleolithic poets

*When you can use in Latin what you learned in science, or
apply the history lesson in English, that's totally cool.*
         — Comment from a former student

I understand what you said about poetry,
that it's the stuff you think of
when you don't have a pen,
paper, or any way of recording it,
that it sidesteps capture as animals flee fire.
And I know that homo sapiens means "man who thinks."
And there haven't been any significant anatomical changes
in this thinking man for 30,000 years.
I understand that I'm no better than him.

But what I want to know is this:
Why did it take us 25,000 years to invent writing?

What did we think about for all that time?
And with no pen, no papyrus, no sharpened reed
to dip in a mixture of soot and glue,
would not what came to us,
what passed through our minds,
would it not all have been,
by your own definition,
poetry?

On girls lending pens

I walked into the classroom and straight to my chair,
But when I reached for my pen, it just wasn't there!
I had no pen! or crayon! or pencil!
I was stuck before class without a writing utensil.

I could have asked the teacher (if I had dared,)
But I knew she would have said, "You're unprepared!"
So to be diplomatic and avoid the fight
I quickly turned to the girl on my right,

Do you possibly have a pen I could borrow?
I'll use it today and have it back by tomorrow.
        "Oh! Furshur! What kind? I've got plenty."
And she turned around with a handful of twenty.

I really don't care what color or style,
I'll take the fountain pen, I said with a smile.
        "Oh, you don't want that one. It comes out all ugly.
And it's made of pure gold," she said to me smugly.

Then how bout the blue?
        "No, that one hops."
Okay, maybe the green?
        "Comes out in glops."
Black?
                "I'm afraid it's having trouble connecting."
Red?
        "I'll need it if we do any in-class correcting."
Look, I said, my voice filling with fear,
Just gimme a pen before the teacher gets here!

        "But this one always comes out in tons,
The yellow one skips and the purple one runs.
When the brown one dries, it looks real icky,
And the orange one's covered with something sticky.

This one's for emergencies (in case I get confused)
'cause it's clean and it's fresh and it's never been used.
I keep this one for quizzes 'cause it brings good luck,
And the ballpoint's splotchy and the cap is stuck.
This one's empty, with the silver band,
And the felt-tip will leak all over your hand.
This one's cracked, and that's gone berserk!
And that would be perfect but it doesn't work.
But here! Take this one! This one's fine!
Oh wait . . . I'm sorry, this one's mine."
I think she went on but I couldn't have cared.
I decided it was better to go unprepared.

On the removal of the antonym section, or Opposites attack

It was a stupid section. I mean, you either knew the word or you didn't.
— Test prep tutor on the Educational Testing Service's decision to remove the Antonym section from the S.A.T.

The Educational Testing Service has done away
with the antonym section on the S.A.T.
Finally, they have done something:
- a) ignominious
- b) calamitous
- c) baleful
- d) bad

Since it only tested the student's vocabulary,
the antonym section was essentially:
- a) germane
- b) valid
- c) apposite
- d) demonstrative

And besides, the only people who did well on it were:
- a) perspicacious
- b) percipient
- c) sagacious
- d) astute

I can't wait until ETS makes the test perfect by
eliminating other sections that test:
- a) reading comprehension
- b) problem solving
- c) analytical reasoning
- d) anything else

May you ask me a question?

Good teachers know which questions to answer and which ones to ask.

May you ask me a question?
If you really thought you needed permission
to ask me a question
before asking me a question,
you never would have found the guts
to ask me that one.

So you think about what you want,
and you think about what you know.
And when you've decided what it is that you want to know,
you raise your hand and wait your turn
just like everybody else.

Like Lilly Like Wilson

I'm writing the poem that will change the world,
and it's Lilly Wilson at my office door.
Lilly Wilson, the recovering like addict,
the worst I've ever seen.
So, like, bad, that the entire eighth grade
started calling her Like Lilly Like Wilson Like.
Until I declared my classroom a Like-Free Zone,
and she could not speak for days.

When she finally did, it was to say,
Mr. Mali, this is . . . so hard.
Now I have to think before I . . . say anything.

Imagine that, Lilly.

It's for your own good.
Even if you don't like . . .
it.

I'm writing the poem that will change the world,
and it's Lilly Wilson at my office door.
Lilly is writing a research paper
about how homosexuals shouldn't be allowed
to adopt children.
I'm writing the poem that will change the world,
and it's Like Lilly Like Wilson at my office door.

She's having trouble finding sources,
which is to say, ones that back her up.
They all argue in favor of what I thought I was against.

And it took four years of college,
three years of graduate school,
and every incidental teaching experience I have ever had
to let out only,

Well, that's a really interesting problem, Lilly.
But what do you propose to do about it?
That's what I want to know.

And the eighth-grade mind is a beautiful thing;
Like a new-born baby's face, you can often see it
change before your very eyes.

I can't believe I'm saying this, Mr. Mali,
but I think I'd like to switch sides.

And I want to tell her to do more than just believe it,
but to *enjoy* it!
That changing your mind is one of the best ways
of finding out whether or not you still have one.
Or even that minds are like parachutes,
that it doesn't matter what you pack
them with so long as they open
at the right time.
O God, Lilly, I want to say,
you make me feel like a teacher,
and who could ask to feel more than that?
I want to say all this but manage only,
Lilly, I am like so impressed with you!

So I finally taught somebody something,
namely, how to change her mind.
And learned in the process that if I ever change the world
it's going to be one eighth grader at a time.

Recipe for a 7th grade boy

for Michael Elliot

First gather the ingredients.

Take one pint of humility,
a generous portion of tact,
and several gallons of patience.
Now throw them out.
You won't be needing them.

In a large bowl, combine:
the memory of an elephant,
an eagle's eye for detail,
the speed, strength, and work ethic of a horse,
the pride of the peacock and the strut of the rooster,
a double portion of the chimpanzee's intelligence
(if this seems like too much, just wait: you will be surprised!).

Allow to cool, and I mean. . . *very cool.*

Stir in a lab's loyalty, the ability of the cat to land on all fours,
and all the cackling loquaciousness of a gaggle of geese.

Sprinkle liberally with the easygoing nature of the mule.
Remove from bowl and garnish with attitude until almost fresh.

Set aside and allow to mature.
This might take some time.

But it's worth it. Because the finished product
will serve all the people of the world like no one else could.

PS — Keep the bowl (you'll need it later for the haircut).

Train of thought

Walking my dog in Gramercy Park,
he looks up and begins to bark,
and I have no idea why.
The only thing in the sky is the Empire State Building.

Is it something I can't see?

She said she couldn't follow her son's train of thought,
which was her way of saying
she was afraid her son was stupid.
I said I thought her son didn't think
by train.

And why should anyone
think by train?
Only going forwards or backwards,
unable to enjoy digression to the left or right,
only capable of negotiating a 3% grade,
incapacitated by snow,
going only where someone else has gone before
and laid down track,
probably Chinese immigrants never mentioned in the book.

No, your son's thoughts travel by different means.
Slower, perhaps, but more versatile
than your ponderous locomotive.
He thinks in blimps and dirigibles.

So go to where he might moor.
Look for tall buildings with zeppelin towers.
Maybe he'll pick you up when he comes by
and you can wave to me down here in Gramercy Park.

I'll be the guy with the dog
looking up at you,
barking.

How to pull an all-nighter

First admit that it's what you'll do.
Resign, and then forgive yourself.
Everything's easier after this.

You will need an extra meal, of course,
so plan it — both the menu and the time —
and work toward it, having it by yourself
when you finally do.

Drink water more often than not
and don't flush until the sun comes up.

Talk to yourself aloud and a lot,
mixing praise with opprobrium —
both are useful in moderation.
Masturbate often if it helps you think.

Kill the clock; hide the pieces.
Promise to start earlier next time.

Things you wish you could do for your brain

for Kerry

Straining port wine
    All the pieces of decomposing cork
    that helped you age and ferment and develop
    such marvelous taste (but which are otherwise unnecessary)
    can be filtered out by pouring your brain
    through a funnel lined with cheese cloth.
    Life's too short not to be decanted.

Washing the windshield, outside and in
    The hazy and exhaustive acid rain
    that coats the panes of your eyes
    can be wiped off with newspaper
    leaving a streakless clarity that will,
    like crystal, chill light white.

Emptying the lint trap
    Roll back the felt blanket
    of what you used to be.
    Clean the screen with wet fingers.

Rearranging the books on the shelves
    Like goes with like,
    biography has no place in fiction.
    Move the brain's big books to the bottom,
    and refamiliarize yourself with the catalog of what you claim
    to know, giving away all you know
    that you will never learn.

What teachers make, or
You can always go to law school
if things don't work out

For every teacher who has ever made a difference

He says the problem with teachers is
What's a kid going to learn
from someone who decided his best option in life
was to become a teacher?
He reminds the other dinner guests that it's true
what they say about teachers:
Those who can, do; those who can't, teach.

I decide to bite my tongue instead of his
and resist the temptation to remind the dinner guests
that it's also true what they say about lawyers.

Because we're eating, after all, and this is polite company.

I mean, you're a teacher, Taylor.
Be honest. What do you make?

And I wish he hadn't done that
(asked me to be honest)
because, you see, I have a policy
about honesty and ass-kicking:
if you ask for it, then I have to let you have it.

You want to know what I make?

I make kids work harder than they ever thought they could.
I can make a C+ feel like a Congressional Medal of Honor
and an A- feel like a slap in the face.
How dare you waste my time with anything less
than your very best.

I make kids sit through 40 minutes of study hall
in absolute silence. *No, you may not work in groups.*

No, you may not ask a question.
Why won't I let you get a drink of water?
Because you're not thirsty, you're bored, that's why.

I make parents tremble in fear when I call home:
Hi. This is Mr. Mali. I hope I haven't called at a bad time,
I just wanted to talk to you about something your son said today.
He said, "Leave the kid alone. I still cry sometimes, don't you?"
And it was noblest act of courage I have ever seen.

I make parents see their children for who they are
and what they can be.

You want to know what I make?

I make kids wonder,
I make them question.
I make them criticize.
I make them apologize and mean it.
I make them write.
I make them read, read, read.
I make them spell *definitely beautiful, definitely beautiful,*
definitely beautiful
over and over and over again until they will never misspell
either one of those words again.
I make them show all their work in math
and hide it on their final drafts in English.
I make them understand that if you've got *this* (the brains)
then you follow *this* (the heart)
and if someone ever tries to judge you
by what you make, you give them *this* (the finger).

Let me break it down for you, so you know what I say is true:
I make a goddamn difference! What about you?

29

The problem

You're the this that somebody ought to do something about.
— Jeffrey McDaniel

The guy in front of me trying to get on the subway
who is blocking my way onto the subway
is not the problem.
He's my problem,
but even I am not so self-centered as to think that my problem
is THE problem.
Besides, he's trying to do what I'm trying to do:
get on the subway.
I recognize him as my brother in transit.
No, he's not the problem.
Nor is the woman in front of him,
nor even the people in front of her.
None of us is the problem,
we few, we happy happy few,
we band of transit brothers.

But there's a guy inside the subway
with nothing but empty space to his left.
You know who he is? He's the problem.
I wish he would look at me and say
"What's your problem?" so I could say
"Don't you mean, who?"
All he would need to do is step aside
and we could all get on.
But does he realize this? Noooo.
Does he know he's the problem? Noooo.
Do problems ever realize that they're the problems?
That's why they're problems.

Which makes me think,
am I anybody's problem?
Am I keeping anyone from getting somewhere?

Not out of calculatedly malicious intent
but unwittingly lazy complacency.
If I knew where to look, would I see someone pointing at me
angrily trying to get me to do something
that might not occur to me otherwise?

New life resolution:
try to be aware of the problem.
If you don't know what it is, it's probably you.
So step aside.

The the impotence of proofreading

For the boys of the Drowning School
52 East 662nd Street
New York, New York, NY

Has this ever happened to you?
You work very horde on a paper for English clash
and then get a very glow raid (like a D or even a D=)
and all because you are the liverwurst spoiler
in the hole wide word.

Proofreading your peppers is a matter
of the the utmost impotence.
This is a problem that affects manly, manly students.
I myself was such a bed spiller once upon a term
that my English torturer in my sophomoric year,
Mrs. Myth, said I would never get into a good colleague.
And that's all I wanted, just to get into a good colleague.
Not just anal community colleague —
because I'm not the kind of guy who would be happy
at just anal community colleague.
I needed a place that would offer me intellectual simulation,
I really need to be challenged, challenged dentally.
I know this makes me sound like a stereo,
but I really wanted to go to an ivory legal colleague.
So I needed to improvement
or gone would be my dream of going to Harvard, Jail, or Prison
(in Prison, New Jersey).

So I got myself a spell checker
and figured I was on Sleazy Street.

But there are several missed aches
that a spell chukker can't can't catch catch.
For instant, if you accidentally leave out word,
your spell exchequer won't put it in you.

And God for billing purposes only
you should have serial problems with Tori Spelling,
your spell Chekhov might replace a word
with one you had absolutely no detention of using.
Because what do you want it to douche?
It only does what you tell it to douche.
You're the one with your hand on the mouth
going clique, clique, clique.
It just goes to show you how embargo
one careless clique of the mouth can be.

Which reminds me of this one time during my Junior Mint.
The teacher read my entire paper on *A Sale of Two Titties*
out loud to all of my assmates.
It was the most humidifying experience of my life,
being laughed at pubically.

So do yourself a flavor and follow these two Pisces of advice:
One: There is no prostitute for careful editing,
no prostitute whatsoever.
And three: When it comes to proofreading,
the red penis your friend.

Undivided attention

A grand piano wrapped in quilted pads by movers,
tied up with canvas straps — like classical music's
birthday gift to the insane —
is gently nudged without its legs
out an eighth-floor window on 62nd street.

It dangles in April air from the neck of the movers' crane,
Chopin-shiny black lacquer squares
and dirty white crisscross patterns hanging
like the second-to-last
note of a concerto played on the edge of the seat,
the edge of tears, the edge of eight stories up going over, and
I'm trying to teach math in the building across the street.

Who can teach when there are such lessons to be learned?
All the greatest common factors are delivered by
long-necked cranes and flatbed trucks
or come through everything, even air.
Like snow.

See, snow falls for the first time every year, and every year
my students rush to the window
as if snow were more interesting than math,
which it is.

So please.

Let me teach like a Steinway,
spinning slowly in April air,
so almost-falling, so hinderingly
dangling from the neck of the movers' crane.
So on the edge of losing everything.

Let me teach like the first snow, falling.

Teachers & garbagemen

They say *Those who can, do, and those who can't, teach,*
which means that those of us who can't teach
end up teaching anyway, just badly.

They say, *Teaching is the Peace Corps of the 90's,*
and I like to think that because no one knows
what I mean, exactly:
whether I'm talking about the weather,
scorching inner-city sons packing urban heat,
dealing with the like language barrier, volatile politics,
trying to convert hormone-driven godless teenage
savages who want to get laid,
or just 'cause I feel like a volunteer
for all the money I get paid.

See, ask a teacher why they teach
and they'll tell you that they love kids,
and Lord knows kids need love;
that they like to be able to see what they're doing;
that it's a dirty job, but someone's got to do it.
This is what they say.

But teachers all tell you they love kids,
because it sounds nicer than Dunce Cap Hat Rack.
See, some teachers *could not* and so they *did not,*
and that's the real reason they teach;
they couldn't type fast enough to become secretaries;
they couldn't type well enough to write pottery;
their pencils are still a few revolutions short of sharp;
their overhead projections are lit only by a flickering fire.
They probably went to a university like mine,
where the education majors had the lowest
average S.A.T. scores
of any other major even though the College of Education
gave out the highest percentage of A's.

So teachers flood the job market with resumes and diplomas
that read like picket and Kick Me signs,
saying, "We might not be the smartest people in the world,
but at least we've got the grades to prove it."
Checking boxes to the left of careers,
they chose to join the ranks
of America's second least rewarded occupation —
after motherhood, of course —
because they were too stupid to realize
that the garbage man makes more than they do.
And why shouldn't he?
He was smart enough not to become a teacher.
And Lord knows someone's got to clean this mess up.
That said, I became a teacher because I love kids.
Sure, it's a dirty job, but so is being a garbage man.

Totally like whatever, you know?

In case you hadn't noticed,
it has somehow become totally uncool
to sound like you know what you're talking about?
Or believe strongly in what you're saying?
Invisible question marks and parenthetical (you know?)'s
have been attaching themselves to the ends of our sentences?
Even when those sentences aren't, like, questions? You know?

Declarative sentences — so-called
because they used to, like, DECLARE things to be true
as opposed to other things which were, like, not —
have been infected by a totally hip
and tragically cool interrogative tone? You know?
Like, don't think I'm uncool just because I've noticed this;
this is just like the word on the street, you know?
It's like what I've heard?
I have nothing personally invested in my own opinions, okay?
I'm just inviting you to join me on
the bandwagon of my own uncertainty?

What has happened to our conviction?
Where are the limbs out on which we once walked?
Have they been, like, chopped down
with the rest of the rain forest? You know?
Or do we have, like, nothing to say?
Has society become so, like, totally . . .
I mean absolutely . . . you know?
That we've just gotten to the point where it's just, like . . .
whatever!

And so actually our disarticulation . . . ness
is just a clever sort of . . . thing
to disguise the fact that we've become
the most aggressively inarticulate generation
to come along since . . .
you know, a long, long time ago!

I entreat you, I implore you, I exhort you, and
I challenge you: to speak with conviction.
To say what you believe in a manner that bespeaks
the determination with which you believe it.
Because contrary to the wisdom of the bumper sticker,
it is not enough these days to simply QUESTION AUTHORITY.
You have to speak with it, too.

Because my students asked me

what i would want them to do
at my funeral, i told them:

write & perform a collective poem
in which each of you says a line
about what i was like as a teacher,
about how i made you reach for stars
until you became them,
about how much you loved
to pretend
you hated me.

*You mean even after you die
you're going to make us do work?*

The body craves

How my heart got to be this way

*The only lie my father ever told me was that when
the time came, I would know what to say to a girl.*

My heart is the size of two frozen hands
cupped between hers,
held up like a bouquet of sensibility,
pressed to her lips, kissed,
held, whispered to, slowly
becoming warm.

Had she ever wondered who I was,
I was the high school boy trying to speak my way
into her eyes, as clear in the illicit moon
as the silhouette of leafless branches
on a northeast night sky.

If ever there had been a time
to say something, it was then.
I could have wished for an alphabet of varsity letters
or spelled out the eloquence of my heart in pompoms.

I know why they say you'll know when it's love.
And the first cut better be the deepest one
because deeper than this heart there's only bone.

Falling in love is like owning a dog

an epithalamion

First of all, it's a big responsibility,
especially in a city like New York.
So think long and hard before deciding on love.
On the other hand, love gives you a sense of security:
when you're walking down the street late at night
and you have a leash on love,
ain't no one gonna mess with you.
Who knows what love could do in its own defense?

On cold winter nights, love is warm.
It lies next you and lives and breaths
and makes funny noises.
Love wakes you up all hours of the night with its needs.

Love doesn't like being left alone for long.
But come home and love is always happy to see you.
It may break a few things accidentally in its passion for life,
but you can never be mad at love for long.

Is love good all the time? No! No!
Love can be bad. Bad, love, bad! Very bad love.

Love makes messes.
Love leaves you little surprises here and there.
Love needs lots of cleaning up after.
Sometimes you just want to get love fixed.
Sometimes you want to roll up a piece of newspaper
and swat love on the nose,
not so much to cause pain,
just to let love know *Don't you ever do that again!*

Sometimes love just wants to go for a nice long walk.
Because love loves exercise!
It runs you around the block and leaves you breathless.
It pulls you in several different directions at once,
or winds around and around you
until you're all wound up and can't move.

But love makes you meet people wherever you go.
People who have nothing in common but love
stop and talk to each other on the street.

Throw things away and love will bring them back,
again, and again, and again.
But most of all, love needs love, lots of it.
And in return, love loves you and never stops.

Time and tears enough

for Sarah

If you had left your home,
left your husband,
even worse still, left your dogs,
your job, friends, life,
left Chicago like a greyhound bus;

if your mother were suicidally psycho,
abandoned by your father,
called every night on the phone,
even worse still, called you at work,
starving, hysterical, naked;

if your class were full of the weirdos,
the obstinate sadists,
and irredeemably mouth-breathing dullards,
even worse still, refused to recognize beauty;

if all of this were happening;
if this were your first Christmas alone;

wouldn't you expect broken glass to bloom at your feet,
little flowers of destruction bursting
like the blossoms of shattered flutes
sown in the springtime of a hardwood floor?

Wouldn't you expect chaos for a time?

When things break, the jagged pieces draw blood.
This, at least, makes sense.
But there is time and tears enough.
So you wait, and you cry, and you cry and you wait,
for as long as you want or as long as it takes.

The girl in the garage

for Rick Bellamy

I'm in a garage in Hyannis. A garage in Hyannis —
Hyannis — which is an ugly word.
Who can help but think of hyenas?
Or worse yet, who can blame me for thinking about Uranus?

I'm in a garage in Hyannis, but I'm thinking about Uranus.
And believe me, I have a lot better things
to think about than Uranus.

I'm in a garage in Hyannis. A garage in Hyannis,
Cape Cod. And I swear to God
there's a girl here talking to me,
or rather not talking to me.
She works here in a baseball cap.
She works here in a baseball cap
with a two foot braid sticking out the back,
jet black. Jet black hair.
She works here and her hands are smeared
with axle grease, hands
dirty as my blazer is blue.
And her boots are as beat up —
Asbeatupasbeatupasbeatup —
as my shoes are shiny.
She drives a wrecker.

I don't.

She says to me she says — she says,
You would never guess, she says.
You would never guess but once in a while I wear a dress.

And I want to say, *So?*
Once in a while I wear a dress, too.
But I don't.

47

I just say, *Yes, I would guess.*
But I want to add,
I have jeans with rips in them, and I have sweatshirts
that I have not washed since Kurt Cobain killed himself.
And you would never guess — no, you would never guess —
staring into the geometric pattern of my pale yellow power tie
that I have at least a rudimentary understanding of most
of the basic power tools.

But I don't.

I drive away from the garage in Hyannis, Hyannis, Cape Cod,
but I swear to God, once in a while
the girl in the garage in the baseball cap
takes it off,
washes her hands,
puts on a dress,
and unbraids her jet black hair
all the way
until night
falls.

Topless photograph of Juliette, taken by Chance Briggs

Juliette, wearing nothing but her beautifully
too-big beltless jeans,
stands facing the grey sky, darker sea,
white-topped waves of the Atlantic.
Her breasts are black and white,
or would have been had she chanced
to face the camera, not the sea and not the sky.
I see her back through Chance's photographic eye.

Chance had this way with women.
They would sooner skinny-dip with him than anything else.
I thought he was gay, but in this photograph I see
it was just a kind of grace that I could never hope to fake.

Juliette is combing the tips of her long and salty hair,
black wet where she grips her ponytail,
and I can see sparkling droplets of water
make their way down her bare back
over chilly and tightly focused goose bumps,
under the rim of denim to where it must be warm.

This photograph has something in it
that I thought or hoped I'd lost.
I think of it and Juliette's back. I think of it and
Juliette's back,
over- and underexposed.

Listen to me:
I think of how, with her elbows over her head
pointing to both corners of the sky,
there would be no shadows on the other side,
no place where skin folds in upon itself.
Perhaps just the smoothest suggestion of smiles.

And how can I help but think of the wind
whipping up the Maine coast,
toying with the delicate tips of the white caps
in the waves of the grey Atlantic.

More than sleep

the body craves
the act of falling into sleep,
the falling takes us farther
than the fall.

I cannot write a love poem
without feeling love, like sleep,
is at last an act of falling,
a putting out of hands
and hoping
never to feel again
that solid
ground.

Playground love

for all the tomboys

You are every playground game I ever used to play.
Every skinned knee, scrape, or king of the hill
exhilaration sweat meets tears in a symphony of salt.

You bring me back.

Every sound I could make:
every yell and scream,
and over here!
or panting hyperventilation
is just another word in the foreign tongue
of summertime for you.

I don't know if I want you to catch me or just run.
So ready or not, here I come.

You've got me frozen like freeze tag.
Please come, please come, please come
and unstick me with a push or a tap or a touch;
it's you I want to be unstuck with.

You're more dangerous than finders keepers,
more stop and go than red light green light.
I want to tug on your heart strings like it's tug of war.
You're good and you're bad like a cigarette in a treehouse.
Or like something found in the sand:
I don't know where you've been
but I want to put you in my mouth
to see where you belong.

Where did you go when the sun went down?
When the summer finally turned itself in like late homework?
Why did we ever stop playing? Let's move the finish line
so nobody's won yet.

I want to take you back and play
with you every game of summertime past.
I want to hide, I want to run! Ready or not, here I come:
I'm it, you're next, think fast!

Going on from there

What my father told me about sex, or The birds, the bees, and the gravestones cemented into our chimney

Dad, this one's for you. Because everything
you told me about sex turned out to be true.

Because you could speak of sex and the penis
as if they both went to Yale,
were, in fact, classmates of yours —
the vagina, a dear old childhood friend
from Holy Cross who used to come
visit on weekends religiously —
because you could do this, it was you
who sat me one day on the hearth
and gave me my Ivy League sex education.

On the hearth beneath the chimney
fashioned out of local rock
except for the gravestones that you found
abandoned in the back field in '66
and brought to the mason, who crossed himself
and asked forgiveness before he set them in stone:
from you, from God, and even from the souls
of the stones themselves,
from Moses Grant, beloved husband and father,
and from the white stone with no name,
only the willow tree in *bas relief*,
pressing itself out.
Sex and death, linked in my mind from the get go.

And like we were jumping into the fire
to teach ourselves to swim,
you gave me the facts of life
as later you would give me the car keys,
teaching me how to drive
when all I knew about the family car
was how to turn her on,
what to press to make her go faster.

You called orgasm the 'sneezy feeling'
and to this day I sneeze when I get turned on.
Is it you I have to thank for that?
And is it your face I think I see
beyond the darkness of my headlights?
Or is it the gravestones in the chimney
that have cemented grief into every act
of intimacy so that it's barely noticeable,
like a willow tree in *bas relief*
pressing itself out of a white stone?

Taylor Mod Squad

He's lost in a canyon and has been for days,
and I can't remember exactly why,
only that Link and Julie were scrambling
over the rocks calling his name:

Pete Cochrane! Pete Cochrane! Pete Cochrane!

echoed through the canyons of my preadolescence
so sharply that I finally understood
they were looking for me.
I was Pete Cochrane.
It was Link.
It was Julie.
And it was me.
Pete Cochrane was the first person on TV I wanted to be,
or rather the first I was convinced I was already.
He was just a clean cut white guy with a badge.
Like my G.I. Joe, the old kind, the big kind,
not with Kung-Fu grip, but the hard plastic molded hands,
one ready to eat a peanut butter and jelly sandwich,
the other measuring between thumb and finger,
like I was this close to getting what I wanted.
I was Pete Cochrane (Pete Cochrane, Pete Cochrane).

But I was Link Haze, too.
It's the part you're seeing now,
the part that's . . . smooth.
Solid!
Name?
Haze.
First name?

Liiiiiiiiiiiiiiiincoln!

Oh yeah, I was Link Haze.
And I was Pete Cochrane.
But I was kind of Julie, too.
With her long blond hair and her half-closed eyes:
I was Julie. Joolie! Jooliejooliejoolie!
When I was Julie I kissed myself all over
and thought about what I would do with myself if I were
Link or Pete Cochrane, which I forgot to mention
I briefly thought might be Pete Cockring
which was confusing and guilty and a little dangerous
and therefore all the more delicious.

The plots don't stick in my mind,
but the characters have sunk their fingers
deep into the batter of who I am,
and I can hear in the canyons
of recollection their names:
Julie, Link, and Pete Cochrane! Pete Cochrane! Pete Cochrane!

Deconstructing naptime

*Marcel Proust believed that he would fly if he could stand
in a corner and not think about a running white horse.*

It is my babysitter, when I was three years old,
whom I credit for my introduction
to the impossibility of absolute denial,
or what Derrida called Deconstruction.
She tricked me in such a skillful way
I never saw her treacherous trap
until after I was already incarcerated
undercover in my afternoon nap.
See, it was getting late in the day,
three-thirty, maybe quarter-to-four,
and I didn't want to take time out to nap.
I wanted to play a bit more.
So she says it's time for my nap.
I say, *Hell no, I won't go!*
with an obstreperousness brought on no doubt
by my afternoon blood-sugar low.
I don't wanna take a nap. I don't need it! I said.
Yes, you do, she said. *Now move it.*

I'm innocent until proven cranky.
If you think I need a nap, then prove it.
Okay, I will, she said with a calm
that filled me with an instant quiet.
You can always tell when little boys need naps
by the passion with which they'll deny it.
If you think not wanting one means you don't need one,
I've got news for you, buster: It doesn't.
In fact only a cranky boy in need of a nap
would try to claim that he wasn't.

Of course she was right, as I later discovered
after years of careful reflection:
the denial of relation between two ideas
inadvertently creates a connection.

One can never deny the existence of meaning
because as soon as you try,
you construct out of nothing the very same meaning
you initially sought to deny.
Think of young Marcel Proust, who wanted to fly,
but never could manage of course,
'cause he never was able to stand in a corner
and *not* think of a running white horse.
How about reaching Nirvana?
Young Buddhist novitiates are told
to meditate, and whatever you do,
Don't think of an apple of gold!

It's impossible! Everything is everything else.
In meaning there is no gap.
There are more things in heaven and earth
than are dreamt of in a child's nap.
And speaking of naps, my babysitter said,
I think you still need one, do you?
Considering my options, I just nodded my head
and mumbled a, *Maybe I do.*
Deconstructed, defeated, and feeling somehow cheated,
I padded off straight to my bed
where visions of golden apples and horses
ran rampant through my three-year-old head.

Labeling keys

Though not a secretive man,
my father understood combination locks and keys.
He was a Yale man, had a love affair with brass
and a key rack as organized as the writing
on the label of each key was neat.

It's the same angel that made him label and date
butcher-paper-wrapped leftovers in the refrigerator
with Christmas-present creases and hospital corners
and a 2 by 2 inch yellow post-it note listing contents, date,
and possible suggestions for future use:
Turkey scraps. Eleven-twenty-three.
Perhaps a yummy treat for the D-O-G?"
secured with (count 'em) two rubber bands,
one for snugness, the other for
symmetry.

But there's an art to labeling keys;
the one you keep to your neighbor's house across the street
cannot say on it:
NEIGHBOR'S HOUSE: ACROSS THE STREET
(IN MAINE FOR ALL OF MAY).
So SILVER CABINET, GUN RACK,
SPARE SET OF KEYS TO SAAB IN GARAGE —
these are labels you will not see at our house.
Instead, my father wrote in his own argot,
in a cryptographic language of oblique reference;
the key to the burglar alarm was THE SIREN'S SONG,
the gun rack, THAT INFERNAL RACKET,
the neighbor's house across the street was now
the FARM IN KANSAS.
VICTOR was the Volvo, HENRY, the Honda, GABRIELLA,
the Saabatini.
A security of the mind, no doubt,
and not so much precluding burglary
as offering a challenge to the industrious burglar,

as well as evincing from my brother and me
much in the way of loving parody,
such as the key to the side door,
which we labeled, *NOT* THE KEY TO THE SIDE DOOR.
DESTITUTE NEIGHBOR'S SQUALID HOVEL FAR, FAR AWAY.
BOATHOUSE IN DJIBOUTI.

Among the neatly labeled keys
(some to cars we no longer have, like POTEMKIN
and GERALD, the Ford)
is a brass ring of assorted expatriates
called KEYS TO SHANGRI-LA.
Little metal orphans, they have all lost their locks; or rather,
their locks have all lost them,
misplaced them all in the same place,
on the same ring, which is a sadness no bolt cutter can cure.

Even the key that says simply HARTFORD —
somewhere there's a door, a box,
a closet full of secrets locked —
and the only thing I know about it is
that it is probably *not* in Hartford.
I keep them all, jingling and jangling,
turning the tumblers of the past.
Who knows when I might not be in Hartford again
and have a need for such a key?
Who here knows nothing of magic that escapes
every time a key that should unlock a door
does?

A year in a day in the life of a dog

In the spring I like the morning,
rising as green shoots bust up and out, sprout
themselves in wet rain and melting snow.
I like to wake up and go out walking
on dirt as black as coffee grounds, talking
about beginnings and puppy dogs,
smelling morning buds being born.
It's true what they say,
morning is the spring of the day.

I like straight up noon in the middle of the summer,
because when you're hot, you're hot, and you might as well run
and sweat your way through bug bites and sunburns.
I like to talk about the heart of things, run
with young dogs and play
because noon is the summer of the day.

And it's late afternoon I like in autumn.
Leaves as red as suns setting, early evening
finally rolling over onto its back for belly rubs and scratches.
I like to sit with tea and think about the ending.
Falling leaves soften the blow, cushion the future
fall of snow. Even old dogs know
that afternoon is the autumn of the day.

In winter I like night.
I think of all my dogs
standing stock still in falling snow and moonlight.
We might be cold, but we're all right.
The winter of the day is night.

The half tail of Winchester, or,
My father dug a grave,
or rather had it dug with a backhoe
in November for Winchester, the family dog,
who was not yet dead

You put an old dog down to appreviate his suffering,
or free yourself of his inconvenience.
       — *Franklin Burroughs, "A Pastoral Occasion"*

Winchester doesn't need this hole in the ground
as a reminder, a memento-mori,
to live what's left of his life to the fullest.
The dog is not yet dead, I know.
But neither is the November ground frozen silent.
Remember it's the things that *can* go wrong that do,
not the things that can't. They don't.
So it is not from lack of love
that I ask the backhoe man
to use what's left of the any-portion-thereof hour
to cut one steel bucket of Connecticut earth
for every year Winchester walked on it
(and that's a pretty big hole);
or that I cover the hole with corrugated steel
to keep the snow out;
and it is not from lack of love that I keep the earth
in an old oil drum —
let me tell you something about earth
and where it comes from:
even if you save it — save every rootish lump and stone —
it's never enough to fill the hole out of which it came alone.
You have to bury something with it
when you finally put it back
or else you end up with a depression.
So it is not from lack of love, but rather
I do not wish the wind to scatter his ashes.

I want to know where he is,
winter, spring, summer, fall.

That's all. That and the fact that, like I said,
the backhoe's been paid for through the end of the hour.
Incidentally you should see the work he's done at the spillway:
Beauty never manifested itself so clearly in a drainage ditch.
We'll be ready if spring ever comes (as I hear it will this year,
right after winter) in all its overcast and emotional glory,
the run-off flows as certain as tears and as sure of where to go.

But you don't think it's fair, like when I say
Good drivers don't even get into accidents that aren't their fault.
But if you ever had to wash the "accidents"
out of Winchester's fur,
caked and stinking, as deep as sleep,
because he was too weak to drag himself
out of his L. L. Bean bed in the middle of the dark,
and was too polite to bark;
had his eyes never been able to meet yours,
as they could not, mine, nor mine, his —
the stump of what was left of his tail
sticking down between his legs —
you would not speak to me now of skinflint love.
Let me tell you something about shame:
It was me who caught Winchester's tail
in the car door seven years ago.
And under the sheepskin car seat cover
the stain of our midnight ride to the vet
still rides a silent shotgun.

Look, I know it's the water in the ground that freezes.
And that six feet down it's always forty-one degrees,
winter, spring, summer, fall —
hence the wisdom of the root cellar —

but what's that other than another indication
that the more things change,
the more the world could care less?

Frozen ground is no more stubborn than grief,
but certainly no less.
So let me tell you something about Winchester:
he does not want his dead body wrapped
in sanctified army-surplus blankets
(made holey by moths and baptized in accidental kerosene)
permanently borrowed from the camping closet,
tied up in yellowing twine
or a bungee cord from the back of the truck;
he does not want his dead body kept frozen
in a corner of the garden tool shed
until the honking return of the Canada geese
says Connecticut is finally thawing.
Or worse yet shipped off to the local vet
to be burned with the hit-and-runs and leukemia cats,
the miscarried colts and laboratory rats
and all because I expected him to *live* through one more winter,
didn't have the guts and forethought which is love
to think he just might die with the leaves,
slip under the falling, white sleep of snow.

Winchester outlived that winter and died in the spring
because I had his grave ready in the fall.
And because it is always easier to prepare other things,
such as the ground, than prepare yourself
for what, like winter, you know will come.

Most people learn their right from left
in one of three different ways, I've found.
Either they learn to hold their hands up like this,
and whichever hand makes the L, that's the left hand.
Or else their mother, or father,
or someone with neat handwriting,
puts an R and an L on the toes of their sneakers
and they learn right from left
as the whole world laughs at them.

Or else, like me, some injury scars them,
either mentally or physically, but
permanently and asymmetrically,
and they forever learn to associate
the injured side of their body
with either the right or left. So this poem is called:

Rites: learning the difference between left and wrong

This was well after I knew some right from wrong
but just before right from left.

To build a foot bridge with a railroad tie
across the stream, that was the plan.
That was the plan for the day.
And I was helping Dad,
I was helping Dad.
And I didn't know it was my right foot
that was crushed beneath the railroad tie
until I was told, over and over for weeks,
The foot you hurt is the right foot, Taylor.
The foot that hurts is your right foot.

The cuts healed soon enough,
except for the one I kept reopening
every time someone like Simon said,
Simon says raise your left hand,
and the railroad tie fell down again
on the foot I hurt which was the right foot.

And now I wonder what other lessons
there might have been in pain.
How many times has a railroad tie,
or some other stick or stone,
left a pain that meant all is right?
And whatever is not
is left.

Stone blaze

We did not scatter my father's ashes;
there are bits that never burn enough
to scatter — bits like bone and teeth,
too hard to be carried away by grief
or any other wind.
We did not scatter my father's ashes.
We buried them
and built a cairn out of the quartz
and flagstone contributions of a wall
with no fields left to minister.
Pine has pushed its way
up through the turns of the century
farms, and everything else.

There is no trail for it to mark.
It stands here marking nothing else,
a beacon to the lost, to assure them
that they are.

Kneeling on the dead needles,
I hold the top rock until I give it warmth,
until it slowly gives it back.

Going on from there

for Cliff, the Wig Man

Maybe 1973 I wrote a note to Mom and left it on her pillow:
Dear Mom, I did not finish my homework last night.
Please wake me up at four thirty tomorrow morning,
And I will try to finish it then.
PS - These stains are tears.

I do remember crying as I wrote the note,
but I remember making sure the tears landed where they did,
afraid at eight years old to trust my feelings to words alone.
Now 24 years later, I have the opposite problem.

I hated my mother's pony tail — gray and beautiful —
sticking out of the gap in the back of her baseball cap,
not because it looked bad, which it didn't,
or because it made her look younger than she was,
which it did,
or even because she wasn't a fan, because she was;
she could swing a softball bat (like a mother!)
and knew every Yankee by name —
had to call me back sometimes when the games were close.
I hated my mother's pony tail because it looked so good,
better than her real hair ever had, she said.
I hated the vain hope her hair let me have.

When you get a wig after chemo and you have gray hair,
you start with white and go from there,
slowly adding gray like pepper to the salt,
which you can always add, but never take away.

She stared at herself in the mirror wearing the white wig.
Oh my God, I look like Santa Claus, she said.

At my father's memorial service, I read a poem about him
and it wasn't until the fifth line where I said
he had an infectious laugh,
but the body of a giraffe — that the Congregation
realized it was okay to laugh.
And they did, discovering in the process
that the well had not run dry,
that there were still many tears left in the sky.

When the wig was finally ready wear, had been seasoned
to that perfect gray, the man said,
Here, I made you this,
and gave her the cap with the pony tail attached.
She thanked him and he hugged her and said,
I hope I never see you again.
Rather a strange wish if you ask me,
but I think I know what he meant,
and may all of his other dreams come true as well.

Sometimes my life is white like a child's note without words.
But I don't care, because you always start with white
and go from there.

PS - These stains are tears.

Grief is a tree

A winter afternoon in the old woods
is a matter of scattered trunks and bright
white snow in battered light and kindling shadows.

Somewhere in the middle of my forest,
the tree of my grief is growing green
because my grief is a pine.

My grief is a pine or a hemlock.
Or my grief is a Douglas Fir, but it's growing in the woods,
a slow but ever-growing evergreen
which must be pruned and kept clean
of the dead and cluttering branches
that seem to reappear with every winter's sorrow.

My grief has no leaves to shed
all at once, but needles instead
that it lets fall all year round
into the blanket of the dead
that sweeps the forest floor.

See, my grief does not so much grow
as overgrow, becoming over time overgrown,
like these trees, which left alone,
soon sprangle in broken branches,
a prickly abandon no one can get near.

I come here to keep things clear,
to make the forest and the trees appear
as straight and beautiful as they actually are,
because, like me, it must be done
or else become undone.

Here in the forest,
even the dead things seem to grow.

Acknowledgements

Many thanks to the following periodicals and anthologies, where many of the poems in this book have appeared:

Bearing Witness; Will Work for Peace: New Political Poems; The Outlaw Bible of American Poetry; Poetry Nation: The North American Anthology of Fusion Poetry; The Underwood Review; The Cafe Review.

About the Author

A passionate teacher and enthusiastic proponent of performance poetry, Taylor Mali is the only person to have won the national poetry slam championship three times. He studied acting with members of the Royal Shakespeare Company at Oxford University and received a 2001 Artist Fellowship from the New York Foundation for the Arts to develop a one-man show based on his experiences as a poet and a teacher. One of the original poets to appear on the HBO series *Russell Simmons Presents Def Poetry*, Mali was also the villain of Paul Devlin's 1997 documentary *SlamNation*. He lives in Flat Iron, New York, with his wife and dog. For more information, please visit www.taylormali.com.